THE WEAPONS ENCYCLOPÆDIA
TANK AIRCRAFT AFV SHIP ARTILLERY VEHICLES SECRET WEAPON

TWE-011 ENG

🇮🇹 THE FIRST ITALIAN ARMOURED CARS

THE WEAPONS ENCYCLOPAEDIA

EDITORIAL STAFF
Luca Cristini, Paolo Crippa.

ACADEMIC EDITORIAL STAFF
Enrico Acerbi, Massimiliano Afiero, Aldo Antonicelli, Ruggero Calò, Luigi Carretta, Flavio Chistè, Anna Cristini, Carlo Cucut, Salvo Fagone, Enrico Finazzer, Björn Huber, Andrea Lombardi, Aymeric Lopez, Marco Lucchetti, Luigi Manes, Giovanni Maressi, Francesco Mattesini, Federico Peirani, Alberto Peruffo, Maurizio Raggi, Andrea Alberto Tallillo, Antonio Tallillo, Massimo Zorza.

PUBLISHED BY
Luca Cristini Editore (Soldiershop), via Orio, 35/4 - 24050 Zanica (BG) ITALY.

DISTRIBUTION BY
Soldiershop - www.soldiershop.com, Amazon, Ingram Spark, Berliner Zinnfigurem (D), LaFeltrinelli, Mondadori, Libera Editorial (Spain), Google book (eBook), Kobo, (eBoook), Apple Book (eBook).

PUBLISHING'S NOTES
None of unpublished images or text of our book may be reproduced in any format without the expressed written permission of Luca Cristini Editore (already Soldiershop.com) when not indicate as marked with license creative commons 3.0 or 4.0. Luca Cristini Editore has made every reasonable effort to locate, contact and acknowledge rights holders and to correctly apply terms and conditions to Content. Every effort has been made to trace the copyright of all the photographs. If there are unintentional omissions, please contact the publisher in writing at: info@soldiershop.com, who will correct all subsequent editions.

LICENSES COMMONS
This book may utilize part of material marked with license creative commons 3.0 or 4.0 (CC BY 4.0), (CC BY-ND 4.0), (CC BY-SA 4.0) or (CC0 1.0). We give appropriate attribution credit and indicate if change were made in the acknowledgments field. Our WTW books series utilize only fonts licensed under the SIL Open Font License or other free use license.

CONTRIBUTORS OF THIS VOLUME & ACKNOWLEDGEMENTS
We would like to thank the main contributors to this issue: The profiles of the floats are all by the author. The colouring of the photos is by Anna Cristini. Special thanks to national and/or private institutions such as: Stato Maggiore dell'esercito, Archivio di Stato, Bundesarchiv, Nara, Library of Congress ecc. A P.Crippa, A.Lopez, L.Manes, C.Cucut, archivi Tallillo. Model Victoria (www.modelvictoria.it), for making available images or other items from their archives.

For a complete list of Soldiershop titles, or for every information please contact us on our website: www.soldiershop.com or www.cristinieditore.com. E-mail: info@soldiershop.com. Keep up to date on Facebook & Twitter: https://www.facebook.com/soldiershop.publishing

Title: **THE FIRST ITALIAN ARMOURED CARS: LANCIA 1Z, FIAT 611 AND OTHERS** Code.: **TWE-011 EN**
Series edited by L. S. Cristini
ISBN code: 978-88-93279888 First edition June 2023
THE WEAPONS ENCYCLOPAEDIA (SOLDIERSHOP) is a trademark of Luca Cristini Editore

THE WEAPONS ENCYCLOPÆDIA
TANK AIRCRAFT AFV SHIP ARTILLERY VEHICLES SECRET WEAPON

THE FIRST ITALIAN ARMOURED CARS: LANCIA 1Z, FIAT 611
AND OTHERS

LUCA STEFANO CRISTINI

BOOK SERIES FOR MODELERS & COLLECTORS

CONTENTS

Introduction 5
- The development of armoured cars in italy 5
- The first armoured car prototypes 6

The first armoured cars 9
- The Bianchi armoured car 9
- The FIAT-Terni Tripoli armoured car 10

The Ansaldo LANCIA 1Z 15
- History of the project 15
- Features 16
- Armament 20
- Operational use 23
- Other users 33

The FIAT 611 armoured car 43
- History of the project and features 43
- Operational use 44

Data sheet 55

Bibliography 58

▼ Italian officers show an American colleague the characteristics of the Ansaldo Lancia 1Z armoured car (1915-18).

INTRODUCTION

In this first volume focusing on Italian armoured cars, we begin by presenting the earliest and oldest ones. In the beginning, these were mainly models that remained at the prototype level, or vehicles produced in very low numbers. Among the many, we have dedicated some space to the oldest armoured cars such as the Bianchi, already present in the Italian-Turkish conflict, or the FIAT-Terni Tripoli born in 1918; the text then continues with the legendary Lancia 1Z, a successful vehicle born during the First World War, which remained operational until 1945! It was a massive armoured car, entirely of Italian design. To complete the volume, we will cover the FIAT 611 armoured car, designed and built in 1932 by the Turin-based company and, as was often the case at the time, with Ansaldo. This vehicle was also specifically designed for colonial use; in fact, it operated mainly in the A.O.I. together with its older sister the Lancia 1Z and the L3 fast tanks.

Over twenty plates of colour profiles by the author complete this book.

■ THE DEVELOPMENT OF ARMOURED CARS IN ITALY

The first types of armoured cars, which date back to the period of the First World War (but in some cases even earlier), were normal motor vehicles, equipped with a kind of armoured body and armed with a machine gun. In Italy, coinciding with the development of the motorisation of the Army and the Libyan War, various armoured vehicles equipped with a machine gun, the so-called armoured cars with machine guns (autoblindomitragliatrice), were already being studied as early as 1911. The great Italian industries FIAT, Isotta-Fraschini and Bianchi tried their hand at designing models of this new type of weapon, but it was Ansaldo, with its Lancia 1Z, that created the best vehicle, which combined a more modern construction technique than the others of the period, as well as having an elegant line. The vehicle offered good efficiency, especially in the final stages of the First World War. This honourable performance ensured that Ansaldo's armoured car remained in service throughout the Second World War, participating only in secondary tasks. Then, in the 1930s, an attempt was made to give the Lancia 1Z a more modern sister through a vehicle designed by FIAT: the 611 model. This, however, was born at a time when armoured cars were undergoing a more modern transformation, and the 611 was already old.

▲ Column of FIAT-Terni armoured cars under the palm trees of the Cyrenaean desert.

▲ A FIAT-Terni Tripoli. The diamond pattern around the turret picks up the colours of the national flag, a custom that will last in some cases until the first months of the war in 1940.

THE FIRST ARMOURED CAR PROTOTYPES

The history of Italian armoured cars was opened by the Italian-Turkish war. First in order of time was the FIAT Arsenale in 1912, built in a single example/prototype by the Turin Arsenal. It was followed by the armoured car built by Isotta-Fraschini RM also in the same year. The well-known prestige car factory, in the run-up to the war, decided to make military vehicles as well, and ended up building one of the very first Italian armoured cars from chassis intended for civilian cars.

1915 saw the turn of the Bianchi 'Pallanza' armoured car. Called the 'Automitragliatrice' at the time, it had already seen a prototype built at the time of the Libyan War.

Also during the First World War, the Italian army also acquired a vehicle purchased in England: the Lanchester armoured car, which was given to the Cacciatori d'Africa, an infantry and mounted infantry speciality of the Royal Italian Army, set up for use in the Italian colonies. Far more important was the FIAT-Terni Tripoli (or Libya) armoured car, which was set up towards the end of the Great War and which, together with the Bianchi, we will discuss in a separate chapter.

Born in the years of the First World War, mention must now also be made of the Ansaldo Lancia 1Z, which saw its dawn in 1916. It was destined to be the armoured car par excellence in the years up to 1945, with continual modifications and improvements (although it must be said that by the 1930s this vehicle had already become archaic), continuing to serve mainly in the colonial sphere. More than 130 units were built.

1927 saw the birth of the single prototype Ansaldo Corni Scognamiglio armoured car; a vehicle with an original and unusual shape, it was based on the Ansaldo truck with the 4x4 wheel formula. These 'minor' armoured cars will all be dealt with in a separate volume of our series in the near future.

1935 saw the birth of the FIAT 611 armed with one 37/40 and two 8-pounders. The advent of the Second World War finally saw the development of the last known armoured cars, including the world-famous Ansaldo AB 41 armoured car (1 x 20/65, 2 x 6.5) built in 1941, of which no fewer than 624 units were built. This vehicle was preceded by its progenitor, the Autoblindo Ansaldo AB 39/40, and continued its success with the 43 version, for a total of almost 700 machines of the three versions together. At the end of the war, the Lancia 'Lince' light armoured car was finally born.

▲ The eccentric line of the 1927 Ansaldo Corni-Scognamiglio armoured car.

▲ The Isotta Fraschini RM, was one of the very first armoured cars to enter service in the Italian army.

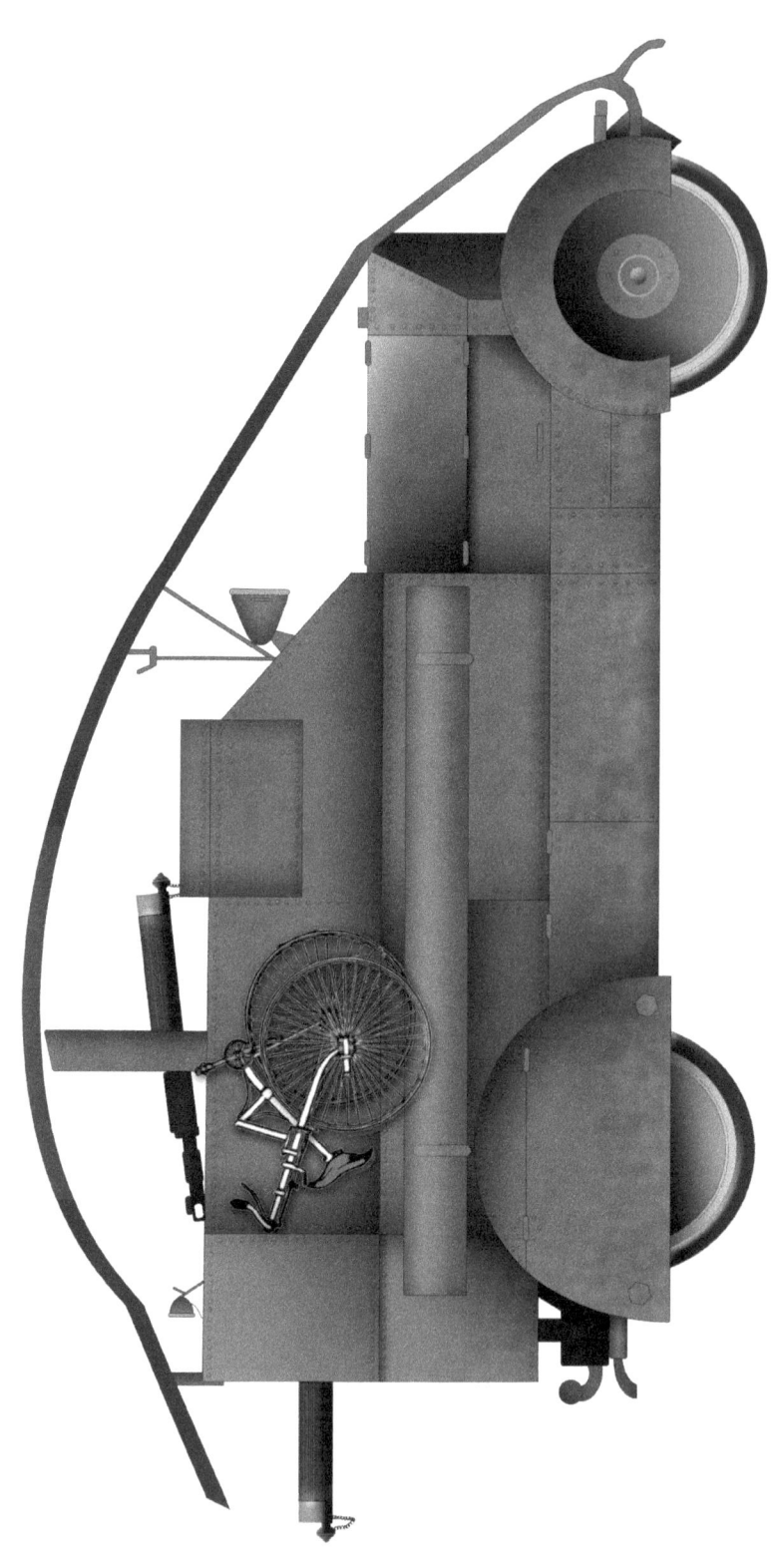

BIANCHI ARMOURED CAR 1915-1918 WAR, EASTERN VENETO FRONT

THE FIRST ARMOURED CARS

■ THE BIANCHI ARMOURED CAR

The Libyan War of 1911, fought against the Ottoman Empire, broke out because the Kingdom of Italy wanted to expand its hegemony in North Africa to acquire new colonies. The Ottomans already possessed armaments and a few armoured vehicles of French and British origin. This led the Kingdom of Italy to try to acquire new vehicles. The Automobile Club of Milan decided to open a subscription to donate two armoured cars to the Royal Italian Army, also with the unconcealed intention of helping the development of automobiles, then in their infancy. The project was the brainchild of the noble and fellow patriot Antonio de Marchi, who set out to build the vehicles by mounting them on two 50/60 HP chassis made available by Edoardo Bianchi and Isotta Fraschini. The new vehicles were 'wrapped' in protective 6 mm thick metal plates and armed with two 6.5 mm machine guns, one placed in a turret in the centre, the other inside the cockpit, with the aim of protecting the rear of the vehicle. The new invention was called the Autromigliatrice Bianchi. The vehicle thus conceived weighed a total of around three tonnes, not a small amount for the times. Special measures were therefore taken to reinforce the wheels. Pirelli also intervened for this purpose, in a kind of patriotic competition, and produced and made available a series of suitable tyres. On the wave of enthusiasm the collection of the necessary funds was swift; not so swift, however, was the construction work, also due to a previous history with the absence of models to refer to. To achieve a satisfactory result, various tests were carried out at the Cascina Malpensa military area, far from prying eyes and foreign spies.

Finally ready and emphatically named 'Desert Cruisers', the two armoured cars were delivered to the Army in the spring of 1912; the Italian command ordered the new Bianchi vehicles to be sent to Libya together with Isotta-Fraschini vehicles and FIAT Arsenale armoured vehicles for front-line testing. No records of their use have ever been found, but by that point in the conflict the fighting was almost over and the arrival of the armoured vehicles failed to affect the conflict. However, as it was May 1913, the occasion of the tenth anniversary of the founding of the Automobile Club of Milan was used to celebrate military vehicles.

▲ A dusky image of the Bianchi 'Pallanza', progenitor (in its own way) of the future Lancia 1Z.

At first, the Regio Esercito was not particularly seduced or interested in the new military vehicle. However, with the outbreak of the First World War and Italy's entry into the conflict in May 1915, the ideas of the military leadership underwent a sudden change, not least thanks to a new, updated and improved version of the Bianchi armoured car, called the 'Pallanza'.

A third model then appeared in 1916, without turret and with the machine gun simply mounted on the hull.

Italy employed a very small number, perhaps four, of these armoured cars along the Italian front from 1915 to 1916. Despite the rough appearance of the Bianchi armoured cars and the small number produced, the model nevertheless had the merit of becoming a forerunner and influencing the design of other similar European vehicles, and above all, it laid the foundations for the design of the future Lancia 1Z.

▲ A nice close-up of the Bianchi 'Pallanza', which gives an idea of the proportionate size of the crew members. In this open-air version, the machine gun operates behind an armoured shield system.

FIAT-TERNI TRIPOLI ARMOURED CAR (FIRST VERSION) IN NORTH AFRICA, CIRCA 1920

THE FIAT-TERNI TRIPOLI ARMOURED CAR

This second armoured car, also known as the FIAT Tripoli Libya, was designed in 1918 and built by Odero-Terni-Orlando, a company for the construction of ships, machines and artillery that operated in the field of shipbuilding and mechanical construction between 1927 and 1933 as a private company, the year in which it came under the control of the Italian state when it entered the IRI orbit. Actual production took place at the Terni steelworks in OTO (Livorno) in 1918. This workshop was one of the first components of the future OTO-Melara consortium. A total of 14 examples were produced, not including prototypes.

The vehicle mounted a 4398 cm3 FIAT 53° engine and had the FIAT-Revelli Mod. 1914 machine gun as its primary armament. Because of these two characteristics, as well as the fact that it was mounted on a FIAT chassis, its full name also included the name of the famous Turin factory. It was the armoured car par excellence used in the colonial areas controlled by the Royal Army during the inter-war period. With the end of the Great War, in which it found no use, the car was sent to Libya with the first batch of 12 armoured cars, where the Royal Colonial Troops of Cyrenaica and Tripolitania were engaged in the reconquest. The Tripoli equipped, together with the Lancia 1Z and the FIAT 15 ter armoured trucks, the armoured car squadrons of the 3rd and 4th Africa Hunters Battalions. It continued to be employed in colonial police duties until the mid-1930s, when it began to be outgunned even in this role and was therefore shelved. However, with the outbreak of World War II, the colonial forces of the Royal Army soon found themselves short of motorised vehicles. Therefore, the few surviving Tripoli vehicles (less than 10) were modified to a more modern chassis. The FIAT SPA-38R truck chassis was chosen for the purpose. The turrets also underwent modifications, and now housed new Breda-Safat 12.7 mm (0.5 inch) heavy machine guns, also salvaged from obsolete Regia Aeronautica aircraft. These upgraded vehicles were assigned to the special 'Babini' armoured brigade in the role of mobile anti-aircraft defence, which was formed on 25 November 1940, but were all lost in the early months of the North African campaign.

▲ A FIAT-Terni Tripoli of the 'Babini' Group abandoned in the Libyan desert during the Second World War.

FIAT-TERNI TRIPOLI ARMOURED CAR (SECOND VERSION) 'BABINI' BRIGADE, LIBYA 1940

FIAT TRIPOLI TECHNICAL DATA SHEET

The FIAT-Terni Tripoli was based on the technical layout of the better-known Lancia 1Z, but smaller in size, and therefore more agile, faster and lighter. The first version was mounted on the FIAT 15 ter Militare chassis, with two axles and rear-wheel drive, a wheelbase of 3.07 metres and a track width of 1.4 metres. The engine was a 4,398 cm³ FIAT 53A petrol engine, delivering 36 hp at 1,600 rpm.

The armoured bodywork, made of 6 mm thick steel plate, consisted of a cylindrical driving and fighting chamber, equipped with two side doors and driving slits, in which the four crewmen took their places. At the front, in front of the combat chamber, was a truncated armoured car bonnet, with side doors for access to the engine and a grille protected by sheet metal fins; at the rear was the tail, on the sloping roof of which was fixed the spare wheel. In the combat chamber was the revolving turret in whose slit was installed the main weapon, a FIAT-Revelli Mod. 1914 6.5 × 52 mm machine gun. In the final version, the turret was cylindrical, while the prototype differed in the sloping turret roof on the sides (similar to that of the Lanchester) and the mudguards on the rear wheels.

▲ The Ansaldo Lancia 1Z seen from the front during the Great War years 1915-1918.

THE ANSALDO LANCIA 1Z

■ HISTORY OF THE PROJECT

Ansaldo was ordered to begin a study on armoured cars after the end of the Libyan War, during the period of neutrality that preceded Italy's entry into the First World War. Engineer Guido Corni, an expert mechanic as well as a connoisseur of metallurgy, and already the parent of the Corni-Scognamiglio armoured car, prepared a design based on the Lancia 25/35 Hp chassis. His design was finished and on 14 February 1915 he obtained a patent on the design files (number 147355). In April 1915, the first prototype was delivered and all planned tests began immediately. After testing, the first Ansaldo Lancia 1Z was delivered to Udine in early August 1915; it would be followed by 137 other machines until 1918. The first 37 armoured cars named 1Z, built until 1916, were characterised by two superimposed turrets, one on top of the other, with the upper one about half the diameter of the lower one. These turrets housed three Maxim 1906 6.8 mm machine guns. Because of this, the overall weight of the vehicle was unbalanced and heavier. To remedy this problem, a new version called the 1ZM was developed, from which the upper turret was removed, and the remaining machine gun was housed at the rear of the vehicle.

Another major problem with the first model of the Lancia 1Z was the armament, especially when set against the poor quality of the armour plating. It was therefore thought that increasing the calibre of the weapons on board would partly solve the problem. The Maxims were therefore replaced by three 8mm St.Etienne 907Fs. The choice, however, proved to be unfortunate as the French guns were not without their problems, being prone to jamming and difficult for the crew to operate and maintain, as well as being very problematic in live firing.

▲ Beautiful colour picture of the Lancia 1Z in the old version with two turrets.

The Ansaldo armoured cars were all designated as Lancia 1Z or 1ZM second series, while the cars produced in 1918 were designated Lancia 1ZM third series. Most of the cars produced belonged to the latter series. The Lancia 1Z, the big, heavy Italian vehicle, proved to be one of the most interesting of the First World War, with high firepower, offset by a mobility not comparable with that of lighter vehicles. It was produced in several examples in the First World War and, due to its practicality, was used until the Second War, later replaced by the new and modern AB 40, 41 and 43.

■ FEATURES

The Lancia1Z mounted the chassis of the 1Z light truck, identified by the name Vettura 35HP-1915 Tipo 1ZM or 'Special 25HP Chassis for self-propelled guns'. Both the 1Z and the 1ZM had the same weight and dimensions; obviously the second type was lower due to the abolition of the third turret, the 4950cc water-cooled 4-cylinder petrol engine was mounted at the front, and had a power output of about 70 Hp and 2200 rpm. The transmission was shaft-driven, with four gears plus reverse, and a dual foot and hand brake system was installed.

The fuel tank was cylindrical in shape and conservatively placed in the centre of the fighting chamber. It had a capacity of 100 litres of petrol, giving it a maximum range of 300 km. The oil tank held 9 litres.

The maximum speed on the road was 60 km/h, with twin rear drive wheels and steered front wheels, with solid rubber tyres and steel wheels additionally protected by armoured mudguards.

However, in 1917 the design was changed again with the abandonment of armoured car covers on the front wheels in favour of a simple wing and also a new radiator fin protection system.

The armour plating made of chrome-nickel steel plates was 6.5 mm over the entire vehicle except at the bottom, where it was only 2.5 mm, and at the tank where it was increased to 5 mm.

The vehicle appeared divided into three parts: bonnet and engine, fighting chamber and turret. The bonnet was armoured car and fitted with fins on the radiator for cooling, the front of the cabin, which was

▲ Lancia 1Z armoured car in the first version with two turrets but already without the front armoured wing.

ANSALDO LANCIA 1Z ARMOURED CAR - ABYSSINIAN WAR 1935-36

sloping, was fitted with a raised rectangular hatch for driving by the driver and the tank leader sitting next to him. All the corner slits could also be opened and closed from the inside. There were two similar large access doors on each side of the vehicle, both with one slot. The other three slits were located on each side, and finally a larger one on the stern for the rear machine gun. Inside the fighting chamber, the petrol tank also served as a bench for the crew of a total of six or seven: pilot, armoured car leader, three gunners and one or two servants.

There was also a small circular hatch on the roof of the turret, the turret rotated on the body on two rings of ball bearings. As mentioned, the 1Z model consisted of two rotating turrets, pivoting over 360°. The first, lower and larger, was armed with two independent machine guns on articulated mounts, each with a horizontal sector of 43° and elevation from -15° to +35°. The second, smaller turret was placed on top of the first, and was equipped with a hatch, also armed with another machine gun. This third machine gun was, as mentioned, moved to the rear in the 1ZM version, and was installed on an armour plating in the rear slot. This gun could also be landed and used by its crew on the tripod in the armoured car.

Above the bonnet were mounted two cut-off metal structures and two complete spare wheels were carried mounted externally on the right side; in time it was preferred to place them on the lower part of the stern. For lighting, the Lancia 1Z had only one large central spotlight, mounted on the front of the radiator. A second spotlight was then placed on the right side of the cockpit.

▲ The interior of the turret system of the Lancia 1Z armoured car. Note behind the gunner the weapon cartridge boxes.

ANSALDO LANCIA 1Z ARMOURED CAR - ABYSSINIAN WAR 1935-36

ARMAMENT

The main armament used during the Great War was based on three American Maxim-Vickers 6.5 mm Model 1911 machine guns. Unfortunately, the supply of these first weapons was never easy, so much so that Ansaldo also had to resort to weapons taken from the enemy, supplying no less than seven vehicles with 6.85mm Maxim-Dreyse machine guns! However, all Maxims, as already mentioned, were replaced shortly afterwards by larger calibre weapons with the French 8mm St.Etienne with 15,000 rounds in tapes. It was a powerful weapon, but as already mentioned unreliable and very problematic in use. In 1924, therefore, these too were replaced by the more reliable 6.5-mm FIAT-Revelli Mod.14, finally providing these armoured cars with adequate armament. All three of these gun models were water-cooled, a fact that led to a great deal of discomfort, especially in the hot climates of the colonies, which forced the cockpit to be loaded with numerous water canisters. In 1938, therefore, a new solution was sought: FIAT mod. 14/35 8mm FIATs were installed on the armoured cars in the AOI. Out of curiosity, light SI Mos. machine guns were mounted on the armoured car donated to Afghanistan. 1918.

For the crew, in addition to the on-board machine guns, a set of four copies of a French-made Chauchat mod 1915 CSRG 8mm machine gun was provided as individual armament. These weapons, however, did not find favour with the crew as they were considered heavy and difficult to use, so in 1918 they were returned to the French and replaced by the more practical National Model 91 cavalry muskets.

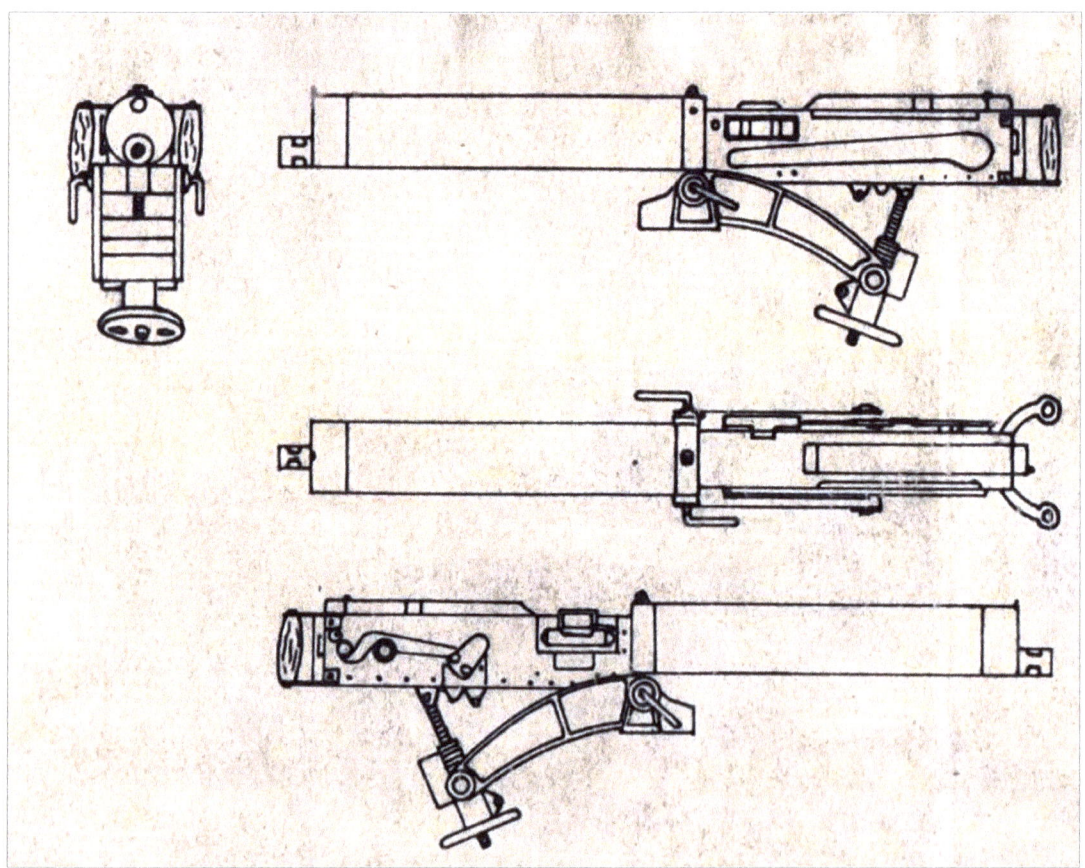

▲ Diagram of the Maxim machine guns, the first to be mounted on the Lancia 1Z. Even German versions were mounted on them, which were prey to the war and were promptly reutilised by the Italians.

ANSALDO LANCIA 1Z ARMOURED CAR - SPANISH CIVIL WAR - MALAGA 1937

▲ Ansaldo Lancia 1Z of the Italian CTV in Spain, on the outskirts of Malaga, 1937.

OPERATIONAL USE - WORLD WAR I

In 1915, the Regio Esercito acquired the new vehicle in a total of 150 units and assigned it in squadrons to the corps and some divisions. The Lancias sent to operate on the Alpine and Karst fronts did some "tests" in the countryside carefully, also because the terrain was not suitable for daring operations with this type of vehicle. After these initial tests, the General Staff effectively abandoned the idea of using these vehicles on the front line. In 1916, some vehicles were used in night-time disruptive actions in Val Sugana. In 1917, they were instead used for public order operations in the Lower Isonzo, contributing in no small measure to restoring order on the front after the mutiny of some divisions of the 'Catanzaro' brigade. For the same purpose, then for actions more police than military between 21 and 27 August of the same year, they were deployed in Turin during the bloody clashes known as 'the bread revolt'.

Finally, due to the disaster of Caporetto, the armoured cars began to make themselves useful, actively participating in the battle, but ended up suffering heavy losses, mainly due to a lack of coordination, with several armoured cars even acting on their own initiative.

It was in this dramatic situation that the enemy managed to capture several of the vehicles, which they later used against the Italian army.

This was also the biggest loss of armoured cars, in fact 10 vehicles were destroyed or captured, with a few others damaged. On the Piave, the army counted only 28 Lancia 1Zs still available.

Once the new line of the Piave had been reached, and the delivery of new armoured cars by Ansaldo had begun, no less than 15 new squadrons with around 40 armoured cars were formed: one was stationed permanently in Turin for the usual police duties, the others all at the front. In addition to their main use in reconnaissance, on the Piave they were often used to observe and direct artillery fire.

▲ Ansaldo Lancia 1Z abandoned on the roadside following the rout of Caporetto.

During the last desperate Austrian offensive in June 1918, thanks also to the dense network of roads that characterised that front, the armoured cars finally had the chance to bring their full potential to bear, and their contribution during the containment battle was greatly appreciated by the commands, but it was also the first time that the command had given clear instructions on the use of the 'new' weapon: the Lancia finally lived a few days of glory.

During the final battle of Vittorio Veneto, the Comado Supremo drew up the first document on 'Norme d'impiego delle squadriglie di Automitragliatrici' (Rules for the use of automatic gun squads), which recommended the use of the vehicles in daring actions of surprise, and the invitation to use the vehicles at least in pairs. In the battle of Vittorio Veneto, the armoured cars were used to exploit the infantry's successes, with rapid advances to occupy points of strategic interest, with the enemy now routed everywhere. This forward rush proved to be a complete success, so much so that all the armoured car squadrons received a special mention from the Supreme Command for their activity during the Battle of Vittorio Veneto. By the last year of the war, the 1ZMs were deployed everywhere there was an Italian soldier, from Dalmatia to the Balkans, to Rome and Milan, to the colony of Libya.

POST WW1

The first post-war intervention took place in September 1919, when the crews of no fewer than 22 vehicles joined Gabriele d'Annunzio's troops in the Fiume Enterprise and formed the '1st Squadron of Armoured Cars of the Italian Carnaro Regency'. The Lancias were always present at all of D'Annunzio's events

▲ The only known Lancia 1Z captured by the Austrians after Caporetto.

ANSALDO LANCIA 1Z ARMOURED CAR - SPANISH CIVIL WAR - BARCELONA 1939

▲ Ansaldo Lancia 1Z, one of about 50 Lancia armoured vehicles converted in 1921-1923 at the Inchicore railway factory for use on the railways by the Engineers in Ireland.

▲ Perspective view of the Ansaldo Lancia 1ZM from above, front and rear (tail). Clearly visible on the front view is the central fanlight and on the rear view is the window of the third machine gun and the vehicle number plate.

ANSALDO LANCIA 1ZM ARMOURED CAR - ITALIAN CONCESSION OF TIENTSIN - CHINA 1937-1943

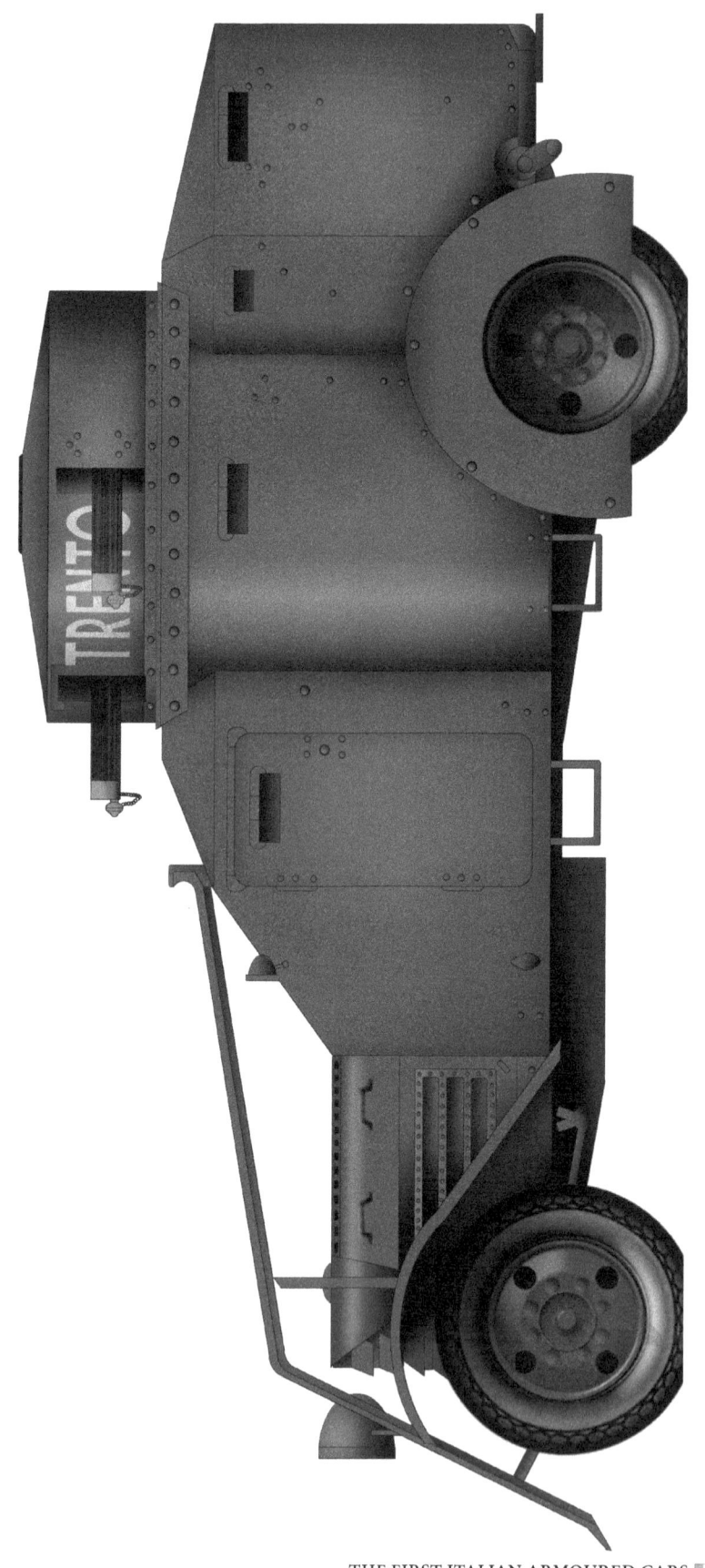

and became a tangible demonstration of the regime's strength. As many as four Sqdr (1, 5, 7 and 15) were part of the Royal Army units that surrounded Fiume in December 1920, but there were no fratricidal clashes. Once the Rijeka adventure was over, all armoured cars were taken back by the R.E.

In June 1920, a squadron of Lancia 1Zs was sent to Albania, where they took part in the fighting against Albanian insurgents in Vlora.

After the tried and tested and effective service demonstrated against the mutineers and strikers in Turin, the 1ZMs found an ideal use in public security and order-keeping duties; they were therefore useful in containing the continuous popular demonstrations of those years, so much so that the Public Security Corps was equipped with 35 Lancias, organised into 7 squadrons.

It is known for certain that at least one armoured car took part in the 'March on Rome' in 1920.

In 1926, after being assigned to the Police, 34 Lancias were also assigned to the Carabinieri and deployed in Naples. Two were sent to the Dodecanese, reinforcing the local armoured car squadron. The Lancias, together with other 'old' armoured cars, took part in the 1919 operations to reconquer Libya, with a section totalling 11 vehicles, which arrived in the colony without personnel, who were then procured locally. This led to some problems and unfortunate episodes in Africa. In 1930, the vehicle, which was considered outdated and obsolete, was included in an overhaul-decommissioning process by the General Staff. The project saw the reassignment of the remaining machines to coastal and territorial defence tasks, especially in the colonies. At the same time, disposals and sales to third countries also began, among them: Albania, Afghanistan, Czechoslovakia, Hungary and Austria; in particular, the Albanian armoured cars returned to Italian hands after the conquest of the Balkan country by the Royal Army in 1939.

In 1937, four Lancia 1ZMs were transferred to the Chinese Italian concession at Tientsin in the Far East, remaining in service until September 1943, when Japan occupied the garrison and finally captured the four armoured cars.

In 1926, six vehicles were sent to Somalia, and mixed crews composed of Ascari and nationals were trained. They then took part together with others in Eritrea in the 1935 campaign alongside light tanks

▲ One of the first prototypes of the Lancia 1Z in the Ansaldo factory premises.

and the new FIAT 611s. In those years, the vehicles also underwent some improvements: for example, wider and more modern tyres were adopted. Although the guns had become anachronistic, on that front Graziani managed to use them extremely effectively.

SPANISH CIVIL WAR

To accompany the units of the CTV (Volunteer Troop Corps) in Spain, a 'spezzatino' of 8 Lancia 1Z vehicles of various types and models was dispatched. They were landed in Cadiz on 5 January 1937, in order to support General Franco's nationalist forces in the Spanish Civil War.

All eight vehicles were entrusted to an independent armoured car company in the Volunteer Troops Corps under the general command of Major Lohengrin Giraud. These vehicles took an active part in the capture of Malaga in February 1937.

Later they were also present in Guadalajara in March 1937. In August of the same year under the command of Colonel Babini, they were sent into combat at Santander and in the subsequent Aragonese and Catalan offensives until late 1938. In Spain, the Lancia 1ZM still proved its adaptability, but the clash with more modern vehicles resulted in high casualties, and at least one 1ZM ended up captured for re-use by Republican forces.

Of the eight primitive vehicles sent, five were lost to combat, mechanical failure or captured by the enemy. Only three (one double turret and two single turret examples) were still operational in February 1939, when they were seen parading in Barcelona.

Now decrepit, these last machines were left to the Spanish authorities, but nothing has been heard of them since. They were probably destroyed shortly afterwards. The lessons generated by the use of the 1ZM and the Spanish Civil War in general would be put to good use at home in the creation of a standard replacement armoured car for the army.

▲ Lancia 1Z and Lancia 1ZM armoured cars deployed in Spain in a ceremonial parade after the occupation of Barcelona on 21 February 1939.

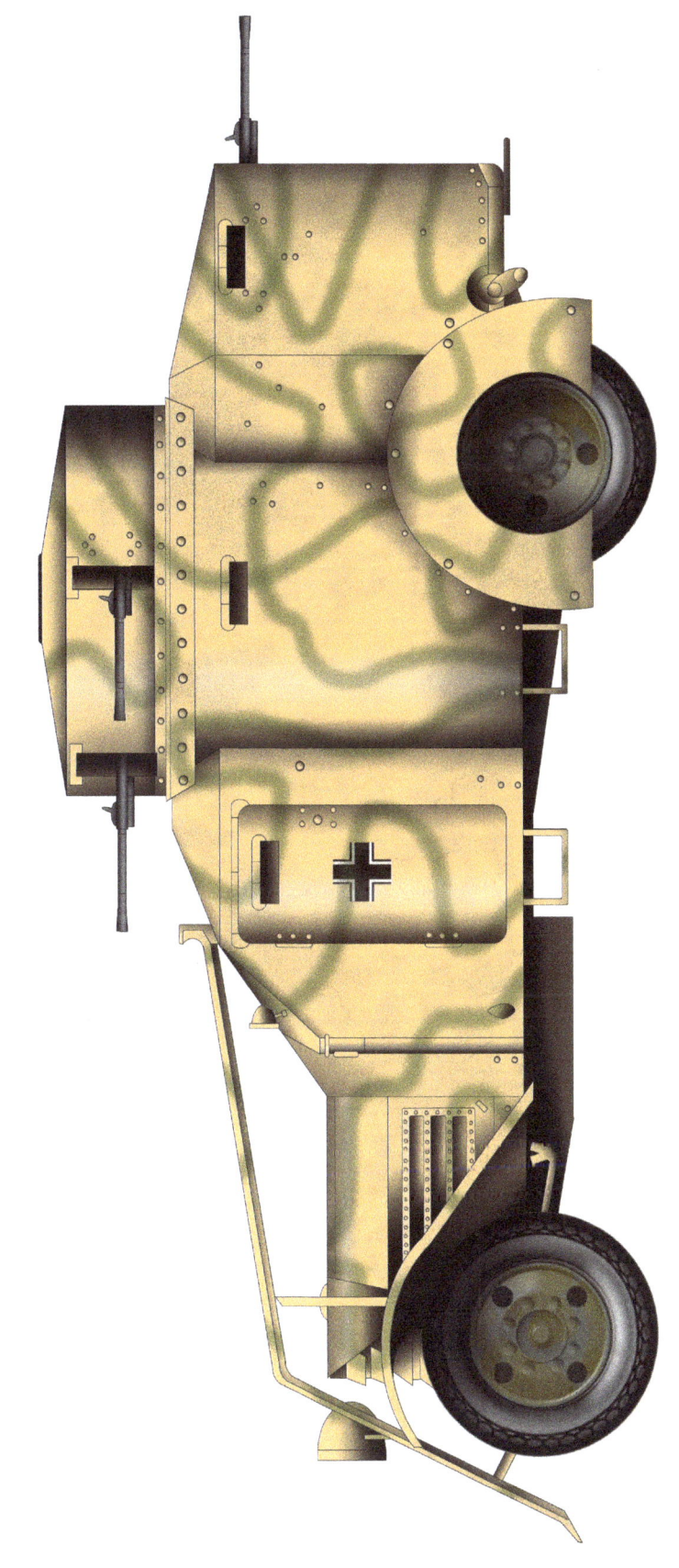

ANSALDO LANCIA 1ZM ARMOURED CAR - NORTH AFRICA (GERMAN VERSION), 1943

THE FIRST ITALIAN ARMOURED CARS

▲ Two pictures of the same Lancia 1ZM armoured car captured from the Italians after the armistice, here in formation of the 1st Battalion SS Police Regiment 'Bozen' in Yugoslavia. Courtesy Bundesarchiv (author colouring).

THE SECOND WORLD WAR

Despite being more than obsolete, there were still 34 Lancia 1ZM armoured cars in service with the Italian Army at the beginning of the Second World War. Despite various proposals, there was still no replacement armoured car. Of these 34 vehicles, 13 were sent to Libya in January 1941 and several others were sent to the Balkans.

A platoon was also sent to the Italian-controlled island of Rhodes in the Dodecanese, to reinforce the islands' weak armoured division. The last known use by Italian forces of the Lancia 1Z was in September 1943 in China, where the vehicles served as a defence force against the Japanese in the Italian concession at Tianjin.

All other Lancias were mainly used in AOI (where they had already been since the Abyssinian War) and here they obviously did what they could in that huge, remote and abandoned theatre of operations. The previous conquest of Somaliland in 1940 was the last bloodless 'ride' for the old Lancia 1Z!

The Lancia 1Z actually survived in use with the Italian army until the armistice in September 1943, after which the remaining examples were all reused in some way by the German forces in the Balkans until the end of the war, which they did with every means they could get the Italians. The 1ZM remained a well-armed armoured car based on a robust chassis throughout its history, but it was simply too slow and ridiculously armoured to be of any real use during the Second World War.

OTHER USERS

In addition to the vehicles supplied to the army, especially after the First World War, some machines were also assigned to the Royal Carabinieri, in 34 examples, and 35 to the Royal Guards, later inherited by the party MVSN. These vehicles were recognisable by their coats of arms painted on the turret.

Among the foreign states that acquired or came into possession of the vehicles in various ways, we would like to mention those that were sold to Albania, whose only armoured force they constituted for years.

One was donated by the Italian government to Afghanistan, supplied with the national colours green, red and black painted on the turret and armed with the unusual SIA Mod. 1918 machine guns. This curious vehicle is now one of the few survivors and is kept in a German museum.

Four armoured cars armed the garrison of the Italian Tianjin Concession. This was a little-known Italian colonial possession in China, administered by the Kingdom of Italy between 1901 and 1943.

Eight armoured cars were used by the Italians during the Spanish Civil War; they were landed in Cadiz and then used in the conquest of Malaga and later in the Battle of Guadalajara, finally appearing in the final celebratory parades held after the Nationalist victory. But by that time these machines were already obsolete and then partly left to Franco's army.

Some vehicles ended up being captured in the First World War and redeployed by Austria and Germany. After the war, some vehicles ended up in the hands of Czechoslovakia and Hungary as well as the new Austrian state. During the Second World War it was still in service mainly in the colonies: in Libya, Italian East Africa and the Dodecanese. After 8 September 1943, the few examples still in service on Italian and European territory were all requisitioned and re-used by the Wehrmacht (see on the previous page the one used by the 1st Battalion of the Polizeiregiment 'Bozen') mainly in convoy escort and anti-partisan combat. The vehicle was renamed Pz.Sp.Wg.Lancia 1ZM(i).

Curiously, we also remember about 50 (?) Lancia armoured vehicles converted in 1921-1923 at the Inchicore railway factory for use on the railways by the Engineers in Ireland.

▲ Again the Lancia 1ZM armoured car of the 1ˢᵗ Battalion SS Police Regiment 'Bozen' in Yugoslavia.

▼ Two of the 1ZM armoured cars stationed in Rhodes seen after an action in September 1943. Captured and observed by German personnel. The vehicle in the foreground has lost its right front wheel (Archive A. Lopez).

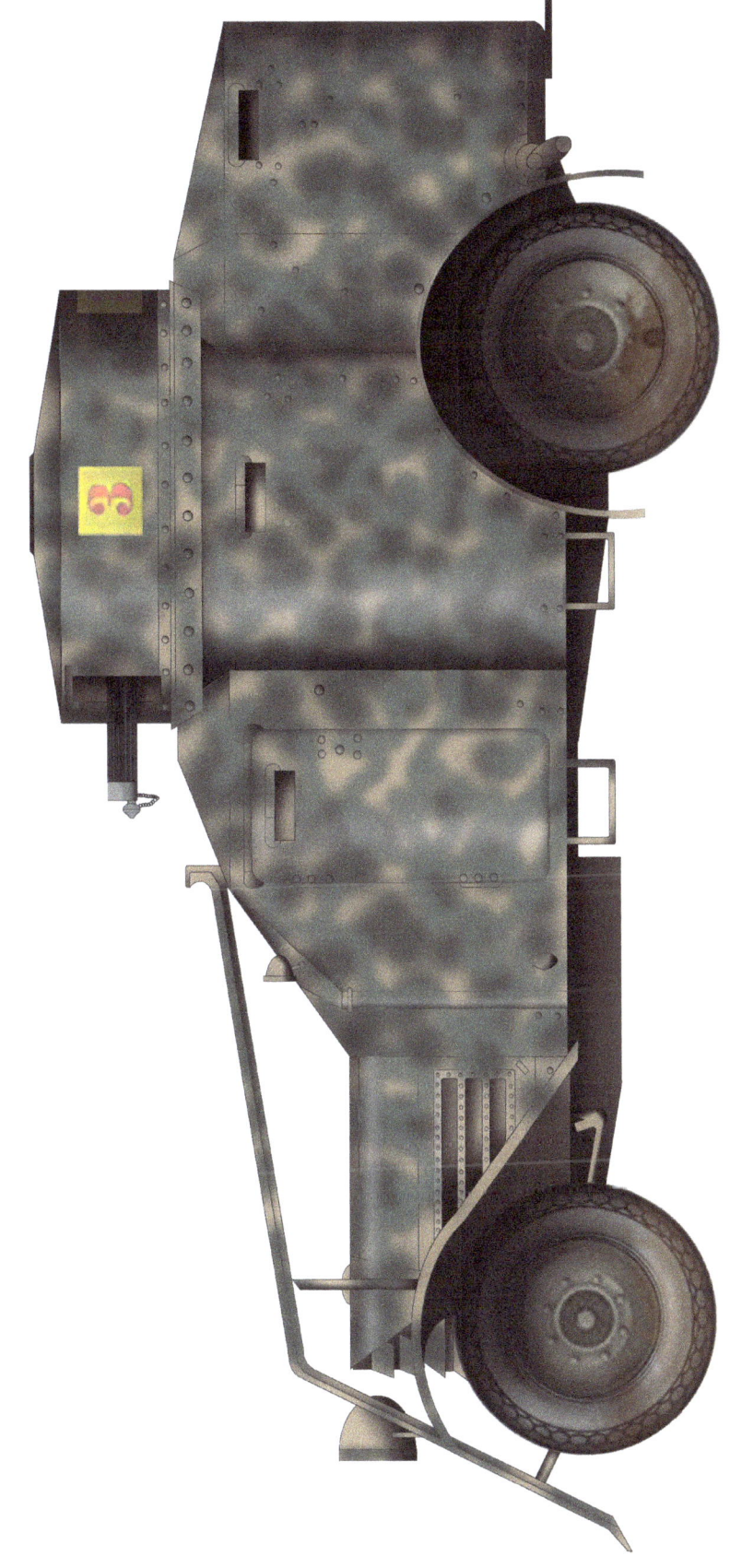

ANSALDO LANCIA 1ZM ARMOURED CAR - CCCXII TANK BATTALION AT RHODES DODECANESE, 1943

▲ An Ansaldo Lancia 1Z with Italian soldiers at the end of World War I or perhaps during the Fiume expedition.
▼ View of one of the few remaining examples of the Lancia 1Z. Museo de Henriquez, Trieste. Foti Archive.

ANSALDO LANCIA 1ZM ARMOURED CAR - 1ST BATTALION OF POLIZEIREGIMENT 'BOZEN', 1943

▲ One of the Lancia 1ZM armoured cars supplied to the Czech volunteer troops who fought for the Italian army and were granted to the new Czechoslovak republic at the end of the war.

COLORI E MIMETICHE REGIO ESERCITO WW2

verde medio chiaro 1936-1943 mimetico	grigio verde 1936-1945 fondo	bruno rossiccio 1936-1943 fondo	sabbia chiaro 1941-1945 fondo	sabbia scuro 1943-1945 fondo	sabbia alternativo 1941-1945 fondo	verde scuro 1936-1943 mimetico
gun metal-cingoli	gomma scura cingoli	panzer grey 1943-1945 fondo	tuta carristi	khaki nord Africa	rosso minio carri	bianco avorio interno

THE FIRST ITALIAN ARMOURED CARS

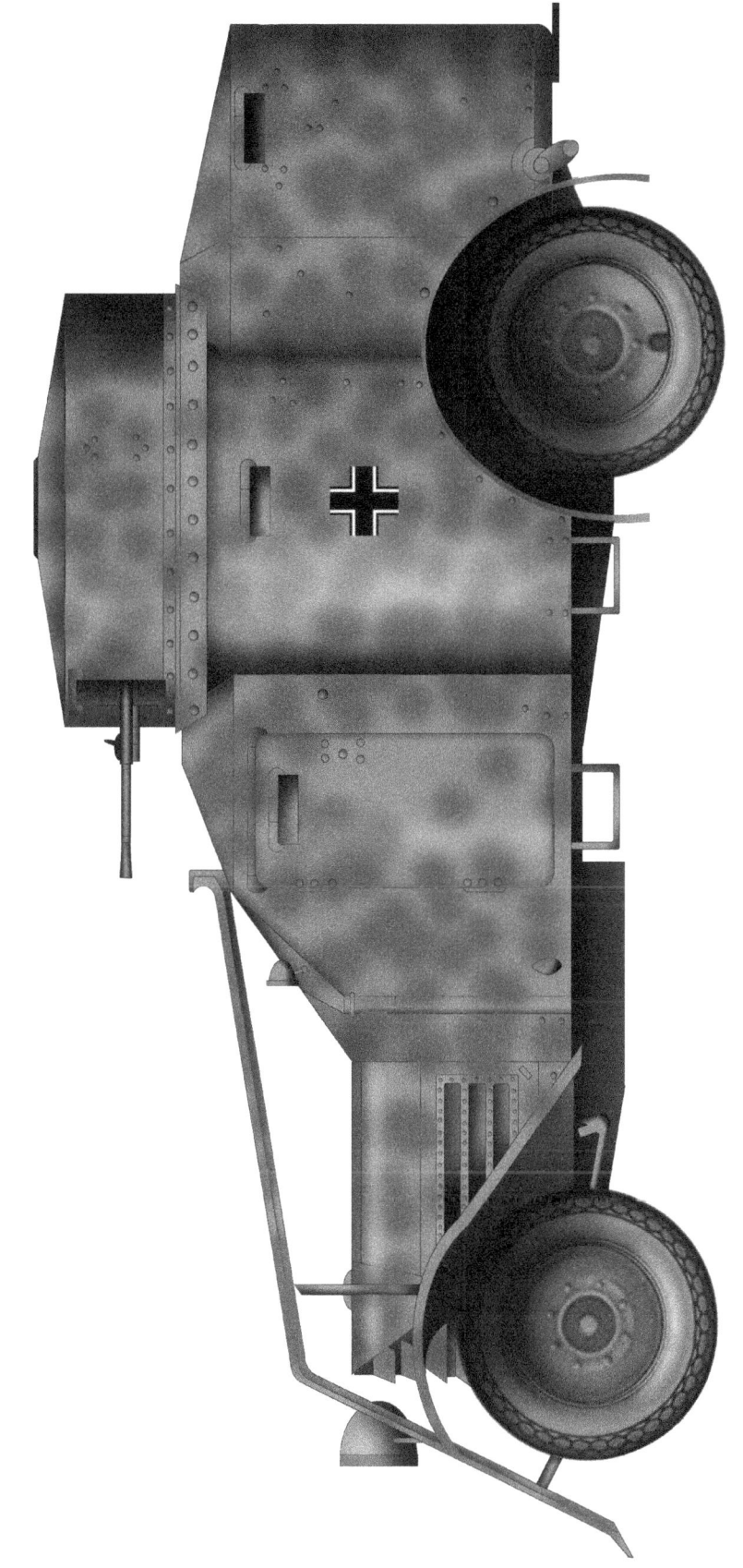

ANSALDO LANCIA 1ZM ARMOURED CAR - IN GERMAN USE IN THE BALKANS, 1944

▲ Picture of the assembly line of the 1Z Lancia at Ansaldo in 1917.

▼ Two views of the engine in the 1Z Lancia at Ansaldo, the 4940 cm³ 70 hp 4-cylinder Lancia petrol engine.

▲ Lancia 1ZM armoured car. Interesting view with the removal of the upper turret.

▼ Interior of a Lancia 1ZM with a nice view of the driver's seat. The cylinder in the middle of the combat chamber was the fuel tank and also served as a support for the crew member at the top of the turret.

THE FIRST ITALIAN ARMOURED CARS

▲ Rare picture of one of the six Ansaldo Lancia 1Zs belonging to the CCCXIII tankers at Rhodes in the Dodecanese. Photo provided by Paolo Crippa and belonging to the Pedonesi family archive.

THE FIAT 611 ARMOURED CAR

■ HISTORY OF THE PROJECT AND CHARACTERISTICS

Nei By the early 1930s, it was thought that the glorious Lancia 1Z had had its day, and a new design had been in the works at FIAT for some time. Designed by Ansaldo in 1932 around the FIAT 611 C (Colonial) truck, which was also the progenitor of the FIAT Dovunque 33, it took the name AB 611 from this truck and was first adopted by the Public Safety Corps in 1933.

Two years later, at the outbreak of the Abyssinian War, the new vehicle fell into place. It was immediately sent to the African theatre of operations as part of the autonomous special armoured car section, where it operated alongside the older Lancia 1Z and the CV33 fast tanks.

Unfortunately, already in this first debut, the machine showed its first shortcomings: a very bulky weight, low speed and poor manoeuvrability on the varied terrain found in the colonies. The vehicle then remained in the A.O.I. and took part in the Second World War with little or no benefit to Italian armed forces, demonstrating a design that was already born old.

Based, as mentioned, on the sturdy chassis of the FIAT 611 colonial truck with no less than 10 wheels, 4+4 rear wheel drives and two front wheel drives, in fact that of the chassis remained the only or almost the only truly modern component of the new vehicle. There were also two spare wheels, one on each side in the middle ace of the vehicle.

It was equipped with a FIAT 122 B 4-cylinder 2516 cm3 engine, with a power output of 56 hp, an engine that provided a very low speed, only just under 30 km/h on the road and less than 10 off-road, with a range of 280 km.

It had a particularly spacious cockpit that could accommodate a crew of 5/6 men. It was equipped with the interesting possibility of being able to manoeuvre forwards or backwards with an appropriate dual guidance system, a contrivance that would later be reproduced in the modern AB40 and 41.

The 15mm armour plating was more than double that used for the Lancia 1Z (with this vehicle it shared the design, in part). The engine was placed under the front armoured car bonnet, followed by the fighting chamber. This had two identical armoured doors at the front with variable opening to allow defence of the driver and servant-mechanic at the side. Also at the front of the combat chamber were two armoured car doors to access the vehicle, one on each side.

Inside the personal compartment, several slits opened for personal weapons and firing. On the tail was a large armoured window housing the rear machine gun and rear driver's compartment. On the outside, an inelegant armoured car box served as a wing to defend the rear drive wheels.

■ ARMAMENT

Mounted in the central turret, it had two distinct versions.

The first version, known as the 611A, was based on three Breda Mod. 5 C machine guns, two of which were in the turret and one of which was placed at the rear of the vehicle.

The second 611B version of the vehicle had a heavier turret armed with a Vickers-terni 37/40 Mod. 30 cannon, in turn accompanied by two Breda machine guns, as described above, but placed one in the turret behind the cannon and a second at the rear of the vehicle.

The armament was completed by 91 TS musket rifles for the crew on board as well as several grenades. The standard crew of five consisted of a tank leader, servant of the cannon or machine gun, two drivers of the vehicle, one at the front and one at the rear, and a final servant at the rear piece. The cannon version appeared to be the more critical of the two versions, for this and other issues, the general staff never fell in love with this new armoured car, resulting in a lack of relevant orders. Between prototypes and requests from public security commands, a total of 46/48 vehicles were produced.

OPERATIONAL USE

For the first two years, the FIAT 611 only did a lot of fine parades with the police and carabinieri. With the outbreak of war against Negus, the army requisitioned these vehicles from the police corps and sent a number of them to East Africa. Immediately, what at first seemed to be the element of modernity was highlighted as a major flaw: the FIAT chassis was simply too weak to take on the very heavy 7-tonne armoured barge that covered it, which not only limited its speed to alarming speeds, but also compromised its stability, combined with a more than poor ability to overcome natural obstacles.

In short, the vehicle was limited to being able to travel on good roads. In Africa, however, the presence of the largest gun available in the country (superior even to that of the fast tanks) made its presence worthwhile.

Only five vehicles arrived in Somalia in the spring of 1936. Here they teamed up with the Lancia 1Zs already present and formed our armoured division in the Horn of Africa...

In A.O.I. the Italian machine guns also showed their faults and on at least one or two machines they were replaced with 7.62mm British Lewis guns.

Shortly before the outbreak of war, in 1939, the armoured cars were assigned to the V Gruppo Squadriglie Carri Veloci in support of the L3s.

There are no known uses of the weapon at the outbreak of hostilities with the British. It is only known that in part, these few vehicles were diverted to Libya with secondary patrol duties. After the loss of Africa, all these vehicles ended up in British hands. The FIAT 611 armoured cars were worthless, which is why all captured vehicles of this type were immediately scrapped after an initial examination. The same fate befell the remaining vehicles in Italy shortly afterwards. Unfortunately for historians, no FIAT 611 armoured car has survived to this day.

▲ Italian police department deployed with AB FIAT 611 and other vehicles, mid-1930s.

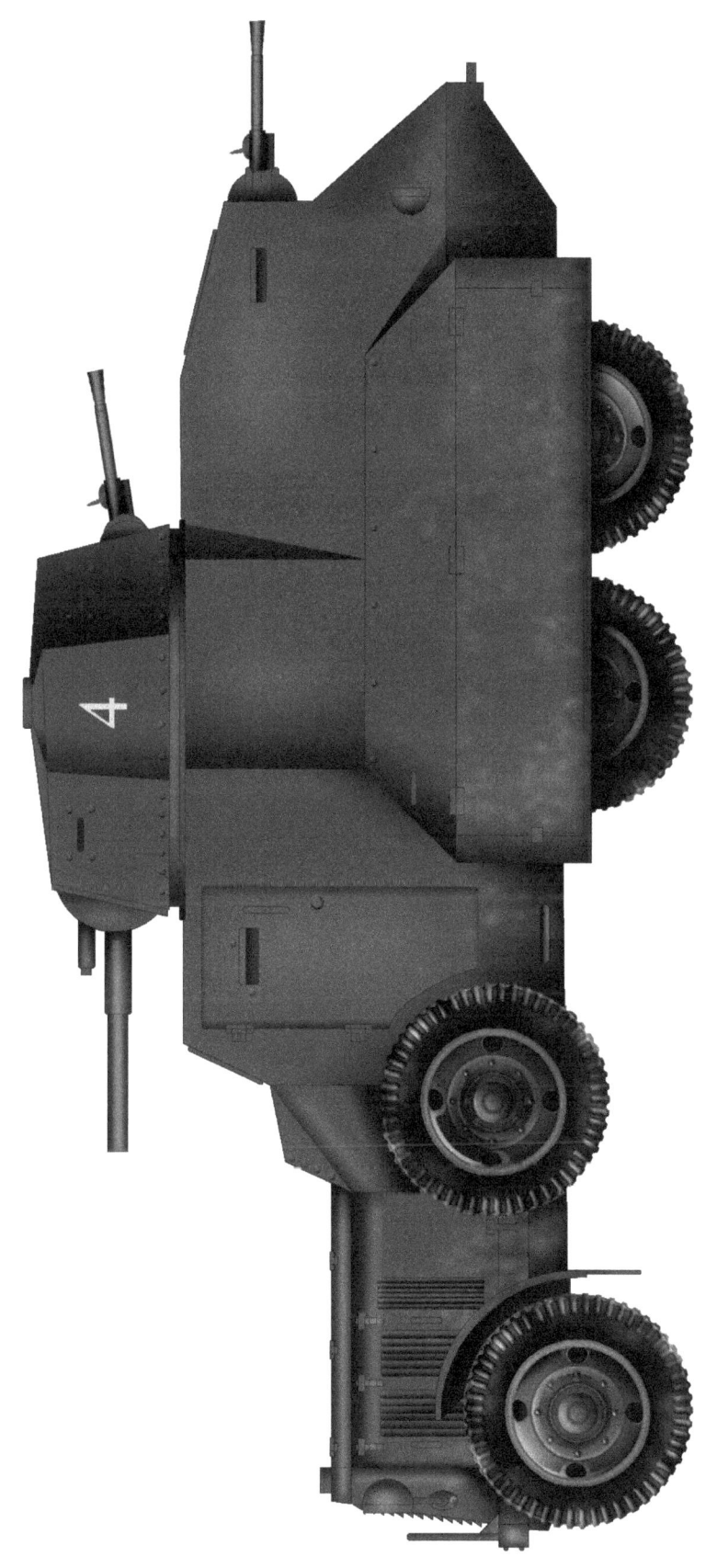

AB FIAT 611 SPECIAL AUTONOMOUS SECTION 'S' IN SOMALIA, 1935

▲ Perspective view of the FIAT 611 mod. 1932 from the front.

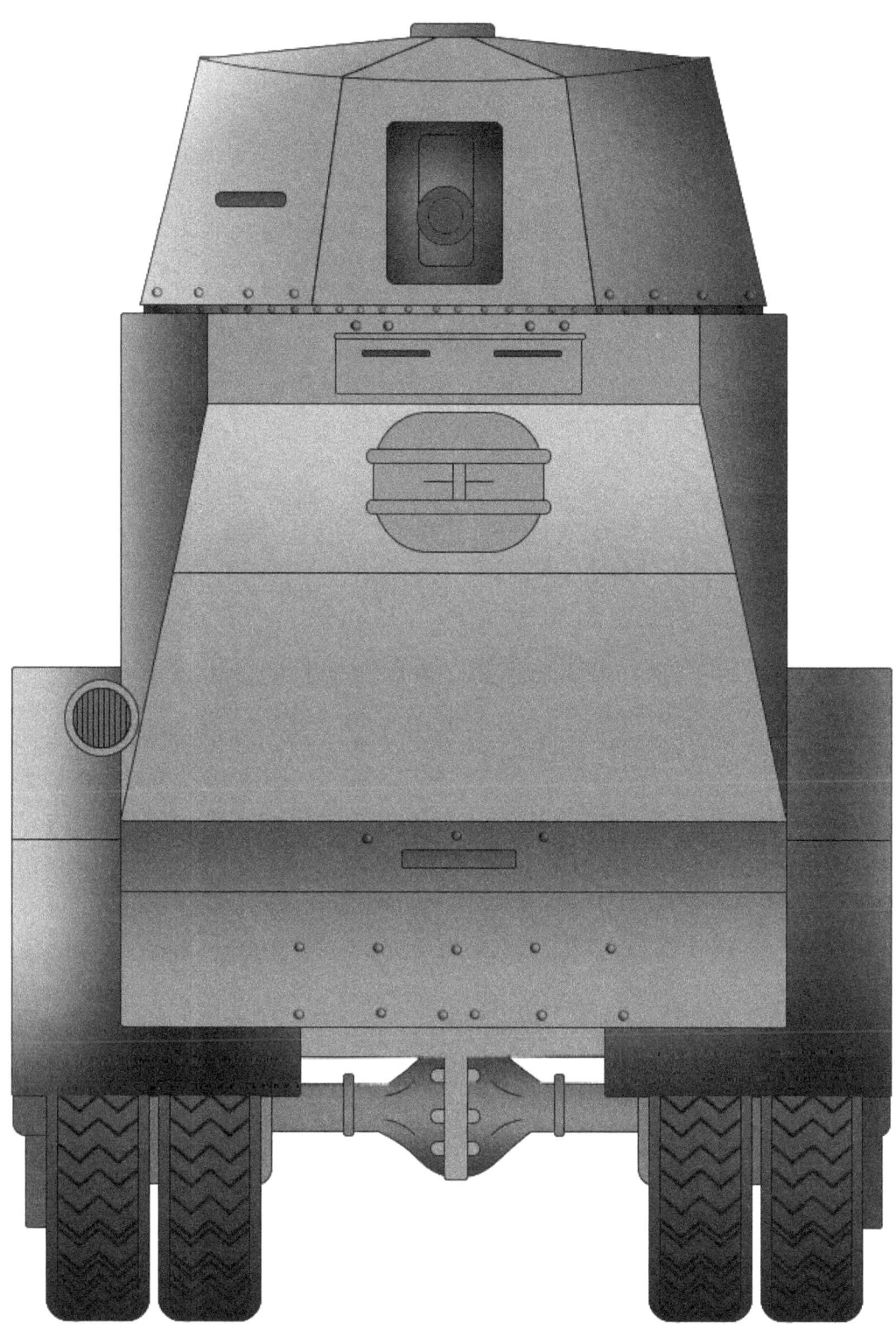

▲ Perspective view of the FIAT 611 mod. 1932 rear side.

THE FIRST ITALIAN ARMOURED CARS

▲▼ Two beautiful pictures of the FIAT 611 C (colonial) chassis used to load the armour and bodywork of the heavy FIAT armoured car.

▲▼ Above: AB FIAT 611 version with cannon in Africa Orientale Italina 1936-1940. Below: the same vehicle to appreciate the 'escape' or rear of the FIAT armoured car.

THE FIRST ITALIAN ARMOURED CARS

▲ For two years after its presentation, the FIAT 611 made only grand parades.

▼ AB FIAT 611 vehicles, probably in an Italian police barracks.

▲ A beautiful view of the interior of the FIAT 611 in which one appreciates the ease with which the crew can work compared to other armoured vehicles.

▼ One of the first prototypes of the AB FIAT 611, during a test phase.

THE FIRST ITALIAN ARMOURED CARS

▲ A soldier has his photo taken next to the AB FIAT 611s just sent to A.O.I. in 1936.

▼ Another picture of the AB 611 B version with Vichers-Terni 37/40 Mod. 30 cannon.

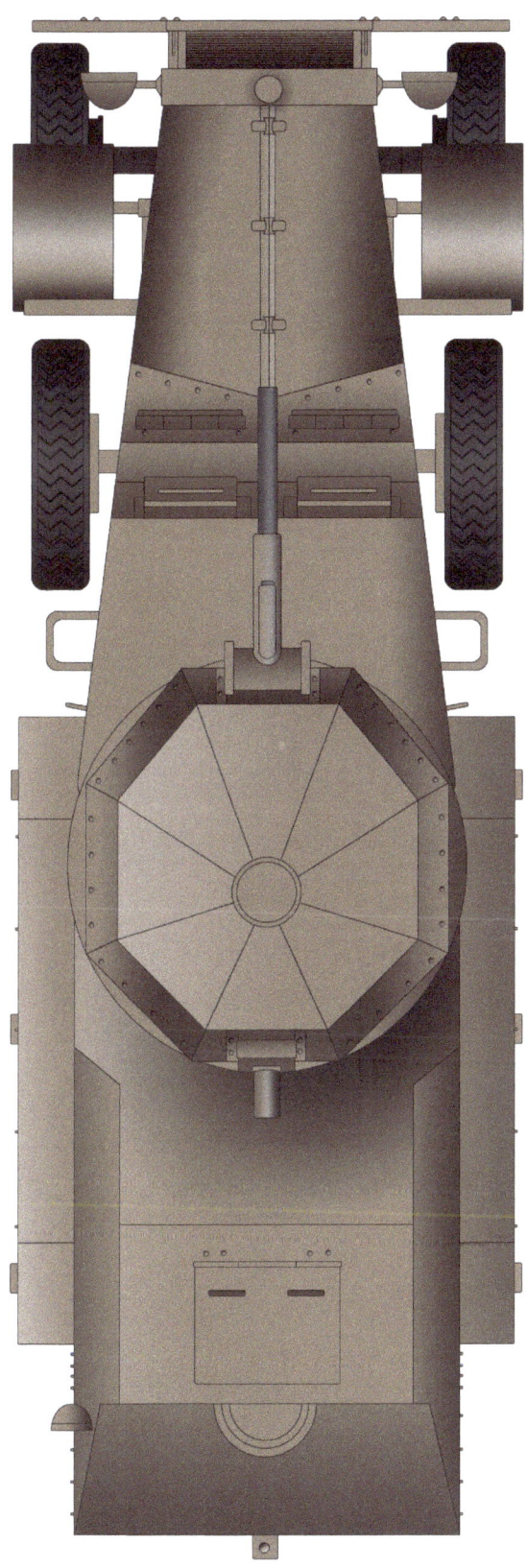

▲ Perspective view of the FIAT 611 mod. 1932 from above.

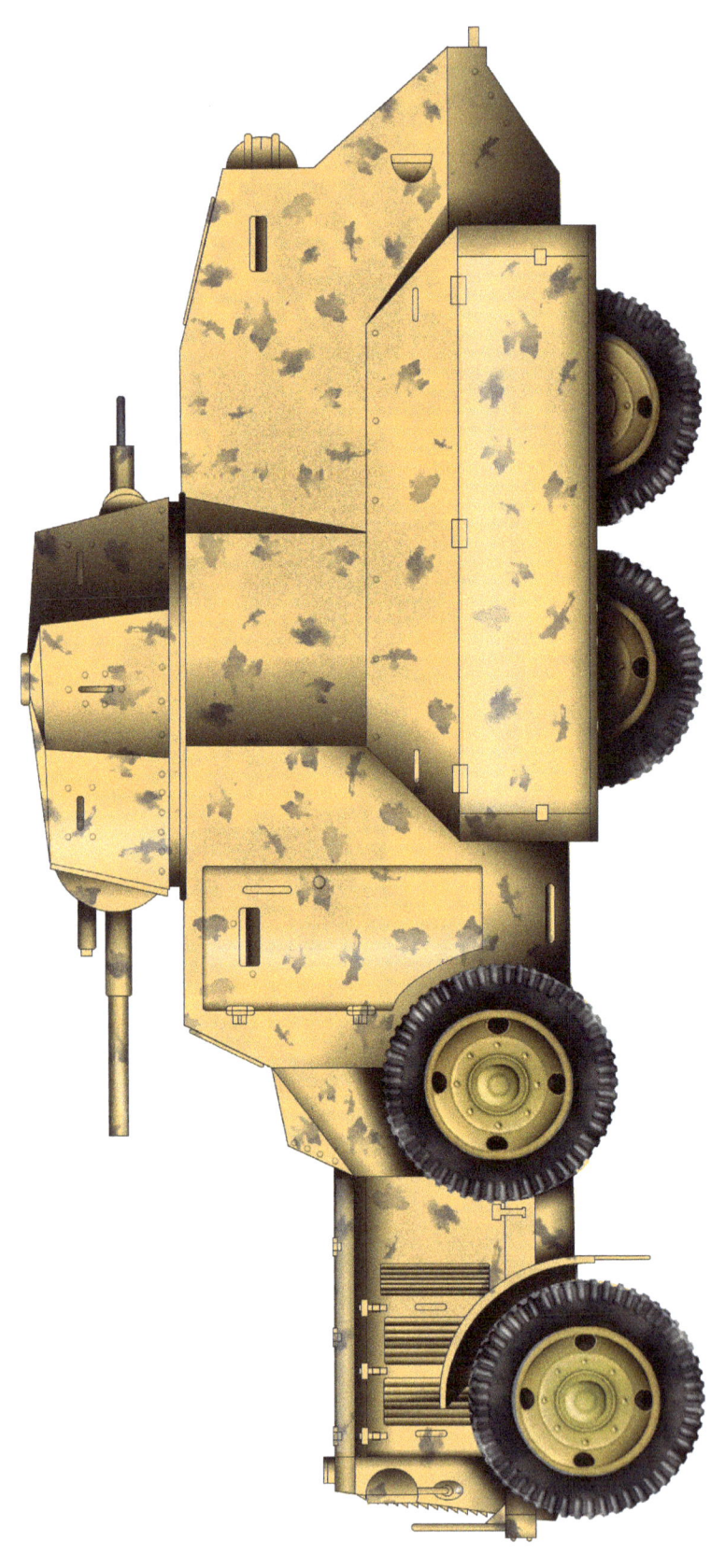

AB FIAT 611 SERVICE A.O.I. ETHIOPIA, 1936

ITALIAN ARMOURED CARS DATA SHEET 1912-1932			
	LANCIA 1Z	FIAT 611	FIAT-Terni Tripoli
Length	5.400 mm	5.600 mm	4545 mm
Width	1.820 mm	1.910 mm	1700 mm
Height	2.400 mm	2.560 mm	2370 mm
Setup date	1912	1932	1918
Retirement date	1945	1944	1942
Exemplars	150	46	14
Weight in combat order	3.700 kg	6.900 kg	1.400 kg
Crew	6/7	5	4
Engine	Lancia 1Z: Lancia 4 cylinders 4940 cm^3 70 hp petrol-powered FIAT 611: FIAT 122B 4-cylinder 2516 cm^3 56 hp petrol-powered FIAT-Terni Tripoli: FIAT 53 d 4398 cm^3 36 hp petrol-powered		
Maximum speed	60 km/h on road 15 km/h off road	28 km/h on road 9 km/h off road	N.a.
Autonomy	300 km on road 50 h off road	280 km on road 50 h off road	N.a
Tank capacity	180 L	120 L	400 L
Armour thickness	6 mm	15 mm	6 mm
Armament	3 Maxim 6.5 0 3 FIAT Revelli mod. 1914 6.5mm machine guns	3 Breda Mod. 5C 6.5 or 1 Breda Mod. 30 37/40 cannon. 2 Breda Mod. 5C	A FIAT-Revelli Mod. 1914

▲ One of the first prototypes to leave the factory in the first version with two machine guns in the turret.

THE FIRST ITALIAN ARMOURED CARS

AB FIAT 611 SPECIAL FOR POLICE SERVICES, 1938

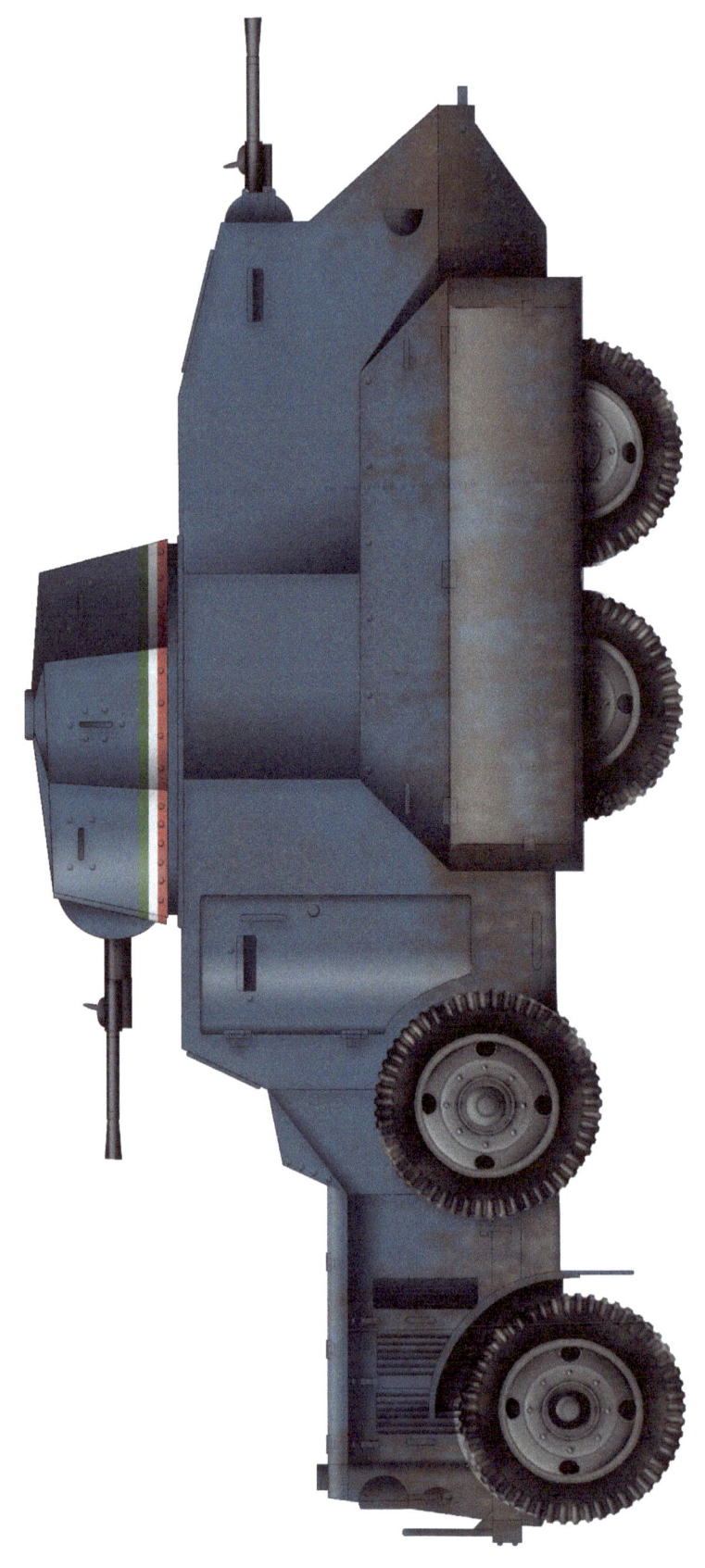

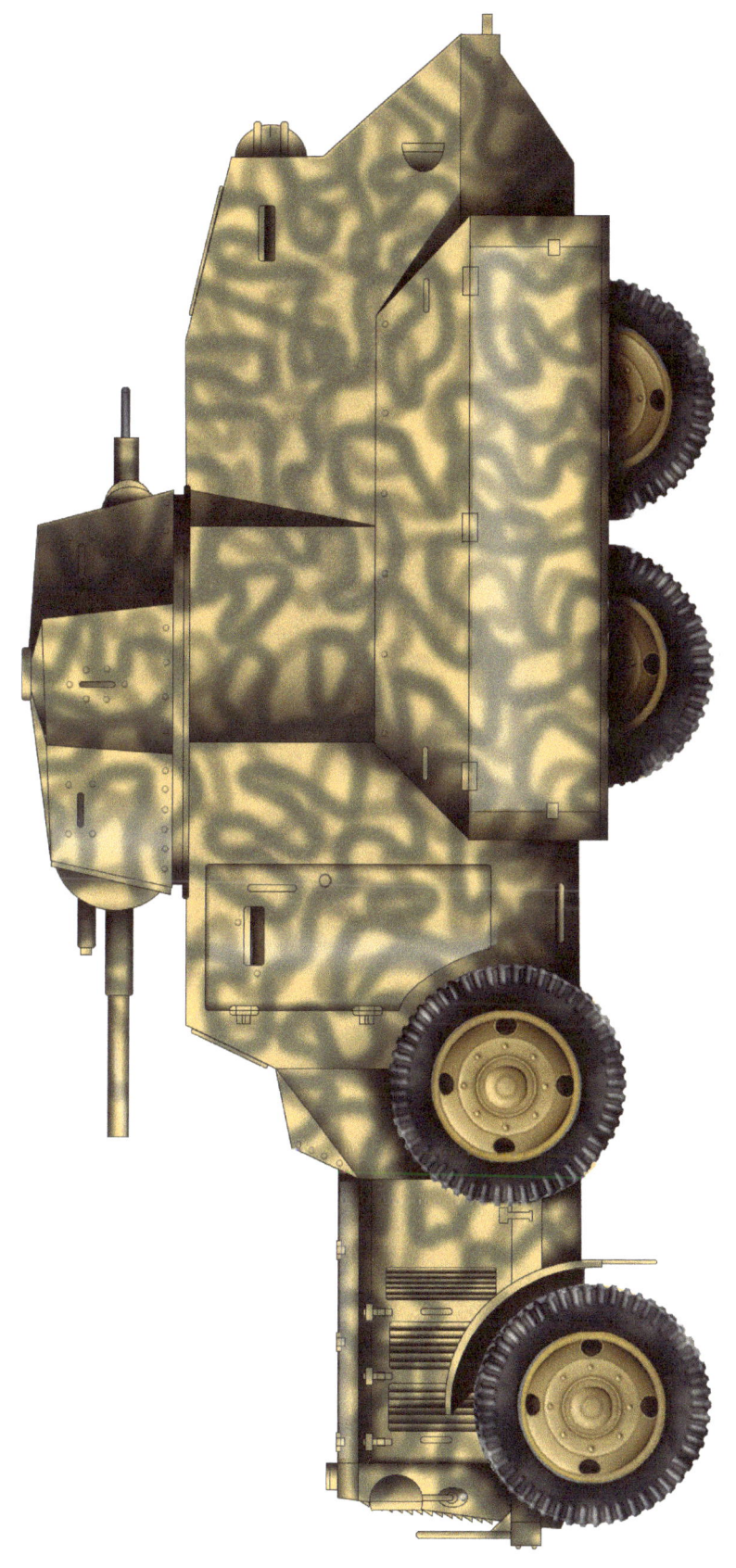

AB FIAT 611 ITALIAN CAMPAIGN - SICILY, 1943

THE FIRST ITALIAN ARMOURED CARS

BIBLIOGRAPHY

- *L'autoblindo Lancia 1Z. E le altre italiane del 1912 - 1945 (FIAT Arsenale, Isotta Fraschini, Bianchi e FIAT-Terni)* di Tallillo Antonio, Tallillo Andrea. GMT Trento.
- *Storia Militare, Le autoblindo Lancia 1ZM*. Di Patrizio Tocci.
- *Veicoli da Combattimento dell'Esercito Italiano dal 1939 al 1945*. Falessi, Cesare; Pafi, Benedetto (1976). Intyrama books.
- *Italian Armored Vehicles of World War Two*. Pignato, Nicola (2004). Squadron/Signal publications.
- *Storia dei mezzi corazzati*. Pignato, Nicola. Vol. II. Fratelli Fabbri Editori.
- *I mezzi blindo-corazzati italiani 1923-1943*, Nicola Pignato, Storia Militare, 2005.
- *Gli autoveicoli da combattimento dell'Esercito Italiano, Volume secondo (1940-1945)*, Stato Maggiore dell'Esercito, Ufficio Storico, Nicola Pignato e Filippo Cappellano, 2002.
- *Corazzati Italiani 1939-1945*, Nico Sgarlato, War Set n°10, 2006.
- *Mezzi dell'Esercito Italiano 1935-45*, Ugo Barlozzetti & Alberto Pirella, Editoriale Olimpia, 1986.
- *Corazzati e blindati italiani dalle origini allo scoppio della Seconda Guerra Mondiale*, David Vannucci, Editrice Innocenti, 2003.
- *Storia dell'Ansaldo 6. Dall'IRI alla guerra 1930-1945*, Gabriele De Rosa, Gius. Laterza & Figli, 1999.
- *Veicoli militari - 300 memorabili modelli dal 1900 ad oggi*, Chris McNab, editore L'Airone.
- *A Century of Italian Armoured Cars*. Mattioli. Pignato, N. (1995).
- *Automitragliatrici Blindate E Motomitragliatrici nella grande guerra*. Pignato, N. (2012). Paolo Gaspari Editore.
- *Los Medios Blindados de la Guerra Civil Española Teatro de Operaciones Norte*, Alcañiz Fresno's editores. Pérez, A. (2007).
- *Los Medios Blindados de la Guerra Civil Española Teatro de Operaciones de Aragón, Cataluña Y Levante 36/39*, Pérez, A. (2011). Alcañiz Fresno's editores.
- *Los Medios Blindados de la Guerra Civil Española Teatro de Operaciones de Andalucía y Centro 36/39*, Pérez, A. (2007). Alcañiz Fresno's editores.
- *Blindados Italianos en el Ejército de Franco (1936-1939)*. Franco, L., García, J. (2009). Galland Books.
- *Ruote in divisa, I veicoli militari italiani 1900-1987*; Brizio Pignacca; Giorgio Nada Editore, 1989
- *Gli autoveicoli tattici e logistici del Regio Esercito Italiano fino al 1943*; Nicola Pignato, Filippo Cappellano; tom II; Stato Maggiore dell'Esercito, Ufficio Storico, 2005
- *I "dovunque" FIAT, SPA e Breda*; Nicola Pignato; T.&T. Edizioni, 2006.
- *La riconquista della Libia*, Emilio Bonaiti, ICSM.

BOOKS ALREADY PUBLISHED

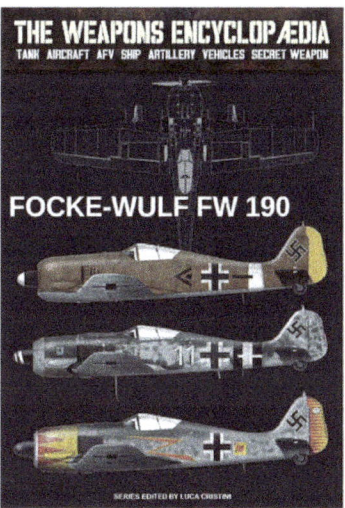

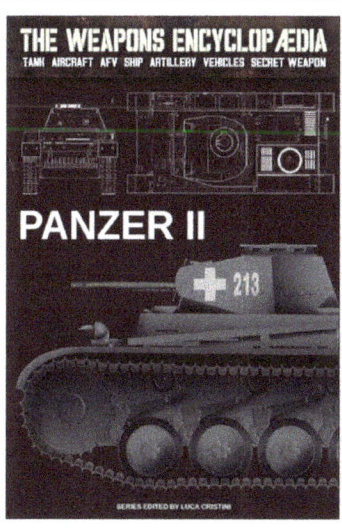

TWE-011 EN

www.ingramcontent.com/pod-product-compliance
Lightning Source LLC
LaVergne TN
LVHW070524070526
838199LV00072B/6694